BROKE-OLOGY

BY
NATHAN LOUIS JACKSON

★

★

DRAMATISTS
PLAY SERVICE
INC.

BROKE-OLOGY received its world premiere at the Williamstown Theatre Festival in Williamstown, Massachusetts, on July 9, 2008. It was directed by Thomas Kail; the set design was by Donyale Werle; the costume design was by Emily Rebholz; the lighting design was by Mark Simpson; the sound design was by Jill BC DuBoff; the production stage manager was Brandon Kahn; the production manager was Jim D'Asaro; and the casting was by MelCap Casting. The cast was as follows:

ENNIS KING .... Francois Battiste
SONIA KING .... April Yvette Thompson
MALCOLM KING .... Gaius Charles
WILLIAM KING .... Wendell Pierce

BROKE-OLOGY received its New York premiere at the Mitzi E. Newhouse Theater on October 5, 2009. It was directed by Thomas Kail; the set design was by Donyale Werle; the costume design was by Emily Rebholz; the lighting design was by Mark Simpson; and the sound design was by Jill BC DuBoff. The cast was as follows:

ENNIS KING .... Francois Battiste
SONIA KING .... Crystal A. Dickinson
MALCOLM KING .... Alano Miller
WILLIAM KING .... Wendell Pierce

CHARACTERS

ENNIS KING

SONIA KING

MALCOLM KING

WILLIAM KING

PLACE

The King household.

TIME

The early eighties and twenty-six years later.

BROKE-OLOGY

ACT ONE

Lights up on King household; it's the early eighties. Sonia sits on the couch painting T-shirts. She is nine months pregnant, about to give birth. Enter William dressed in work clothes.

WILLIAM. Hey, baby doll. *(Sonia tries to cover the shirts.)*
SONIA. Don't look.
WILLIAM. What?
SONIA. Don't look. Don't look. Turn around.
WILLIAM. Why?
SONIA. William, turn your behind around.
WILLIAM. Alright. I'm turning. *(William turns.)*
SONIA. Why are you home?
WILLIAM. Same old thing. Bastards didn't want to give me any overtime. So I'm home.
SONIA. That's not good.
WILLIAM. I can go somewhere else if you want.
SONIA. I don't want you anywhere except with me, but we could use the extra money.
WILLIAM. We're fine, baby girl. Curtis said he's got some extra work next weekend.
SONIA. Curtis said he had extra work last weekend. But you spent last Saturday trying to get in touch with him.
WILLIAM. He got caught up with something, but this weekend he'll come through. Don't worry. Now, why am I turned around? You had another man in here while I was gone?
SONIA. You know better than that.
WILLIAM. Then let me see what you're hiding.
SONIA. Wait a minute. Do you remember those cute T-shirts we

5

saw at Penney's? The ones with "family" printed on it.

WILLIAM. Yeah.

SONIA. And you said that they were too expensive, and for that price we could just make our own.

WILLIAM. Damn right.

SONIA. Turn around. *(Sonia shows William three shirts: two adults and one for a baby. The shirts are hand-painted beautifully. One has a big "K" on it, one has a big "I," and the other a big "N.")* I just found the shirts in our closet and this is a onesie from the baby shower.

WILLIAM. These are nice.

SONIA. I found the paint in the basement. Didn't even know we had it.

WILLIAM. They look better than the ones at the store.

SONIA. You really like them?

WILLIAM. I do. But if you were trying to spell our last name, then you're missing a letter.

SONIA. I know. Wishful thinking.

WILLIAM. Let's get little Ennis out first. Then we can think about another. *(William looks again at the shirts.)*

SONIA. I know the onesie is a little big for a newborn, but it will be perfect for Christmas. Santa's first gift to the baby.

WILLIAM. Santa? I don't know about that.

SONIA. William, don't start this again.

WILLIAM. It ain't right, baby girl. My brothers, sisters and I were all raised to believe that Mama and Daddy worked hard to get us gifts, not some fat white man.

SONIA. It's just for fun.

WILLIAM. Come to think about it, unless we have dumb kids I don't think they'll even go for it.

SONIA. Why?

WILLIAM. One. We live in the 'hood, Crip neighborhood at that. You see all these boys around here wearing nothing but blue. If Santa comes through here in all that red, somebody's going to shoot him and jack his sleigh. Reindeer and all. Two. We ain't got a chimney and we got bars on every window. The most devious crackhead on the block can't get in here. What makes you think Santa can?

SONIA. We should talk about something else.

WILLIAM. Why, because I'm right.

SONIA. No, because you're going to get yourself all worked up. Come on. Sit down. *(William and Sonia sit.)*

WILLIAM. You're the one that started talking about Santa Claus and …

SONIA. Shhh. Just hold me. You've been working hard all week. It feels like we've barely had a minute to relax together.

WILLIAM. Another thing about Santa is …

SONIA. I said, Shhh. Just hold me. *(William cuddles with his wife.)* You win. I can see it now. We won't teach our kids about Santa. If it makes you happy, we'll teach them that Santa is inherently racist and sexist and is another clever tool devised by "the man" to further oppress our people.

WILLIAM. Good. What else do you see?

SONIA. Us. Still married. With children that grow up to be wise and live lives that make us proud. And we all live together in a big beautiful house. Not this one. A really big one in a nice neighborhood where you don't need bars on the window. And there's a fireplace with a chimney, so if Santa wasn't a racist tool, he could slide down with gifts. There's no Crips or Bloods and our children can play in the streets. And we're happy together … for a long time … our family. *(Lights down as William and Sonia take a nap. Lights up on the King household twenty-six years later. William and Sonia are sleeping on the couch in the same position as before. They are holding each other close. Sonia awakens. She stands, covers William with a blanket, and kisses his head. She then slowly backs up and disappears up the stairs. She is gone. William begins to awake. He is startled, as if he has had a bad dream. He stands and walks towards the stairs. He stops and looks at his face in the mirror. He doesn't like what he sees. William exits upstairs. Ennis and Malcolm enter from outside. They are carrying breakfast.)*

ENNIS. Why, because I came up with it?

MALCOLM. No, because it's ridiculous.

ENNIS. Don't hate me because I came up with my own science.

MALCOLM. It's not a science, Ennis.

ENNIS. I think it is.

MALCOLM. I know that it's not. That's what I studied. *(Calling upstairs.)* Yo, Pops. We're back. *(Back to Ennis.)* Just because you want something to be a science, doesn't make it a science. It has to hold certain characteristics. And a better name wouldn't hurt either.

ENNIS. What's wrong with the name?

MALCOLM. Broke-ology?

ENNIS. Yes, broke-ology. The study of being broke.

MALCOLM. You can't just throw "ology" at the end of something

7

and it instantly becomes a science. What's next? *(Malcolm holds up a cup of coffee.)* Coffee-ology, the study of coffee. *(Malcolm points to his shoes.)* Nike-ology, the study of Nikes. *(Ennis points to himself.)*

ENNIS. Pimp-ology, the study of pimping.

MALCOLM. I've only been home for a day and you're already making my brain hurt. Look, where's the scientific method? How does one apply broke-ology?

ENNIS. I'm glad that you asked, because I've thought about this for a little while.

MALCOLM. Where are the bones?

ENNIS. The bookshelf with the other games. Anyway, the whole concept behind broke-ology is that …

MALCOLM. Yo, Pops. Pops, can you hear me?

WILLIAM. *(Offstage.)* I'm upstairs.

MALCOLM. I know. Come on down. We got breakfast.

WILLIAM. *(Offstage.)* Alright.

MALCOLM. You were saying.

ENNIS. Yes, broke-ology. It is a complex new science that examines two things. One, being broke. Two, staying alive despite your brokeness.

MALCOLM. Sounds very complex.

ENNIS. It is. And more importantly, very useful. Much more useful than that caveman shit they taught you at UConn.

MALCOLM. Really?

ENNIS. Yes.

MALCOLM. Caveman shit?

ENNIS. Compared to broke-ology it's all ancient. I'm telling you.

MALCOLM. Okay, you've got me interested. Let me hear a few of your theories.

ENNIS. Theories?

MALCOLM. You have to have theories. I mean, if this new science of yours is going to be as influential as you say it is.

ENNIS. Of course I've got theories. I've got all that. Theories, hypotheses, equations. All that.

MALCOLM. Equations. Broke-ology has equations.

ENNIS. Ain't that what I just said?

MALCOLM. Then profess, professor. Take me back to school.

ENNIS. Okay, I'll tell you. But this shit might just blow your mind. I thought of this one while I was in the bathroom. Wrote it out on some toilet paper. Goes like this. *(Ennis closes his eyes as if he*

is struggling to remember.) Fried bologna times sidewalk sales plus minimum wage minus health insurance/adequate education equals Brokeness times being alive. Bam! Broke-ology, baby. *(Both laugh.)*
MALCOLM. You are a fool.
ENNIS. Ain't nothing changed.
MALCOLM. I still say it's not a science.
ENNIS. I know. I know, but what if it was? We'd all have degrees in that shit.
MALCOLM. Masters. Doctorates, maybe. *(William enters from upstairs wearing an eye patch.)*
ENNIS. I'd teach "How to Stretch a Dollar 101." And you could teach "Cooking with Government Cheese." *(They see William and the patch.)*
WILLIAM. Morning.
MALCOLM. Good morning, Pops.
WILLIAM. We ready for breakfast? Dominoes maybe?
ENNIS. *(Referring to the patch.)* Aye-aye, captain.
WILLIAM. You get the chocolate milk?
MALCOLM. I did. But uh … What's with the patch?
WILLIAM. What?
MALCOLM. You're wearing my old eye patch from Halloween.
WILLIAM. I don't want to talk about it. Not now.
ENNIS. You're just going to rock the eye patch and not talk about why.
WILLIAM. Yes. I am. We'll talk about it later. Right now I just want to eat. *(William walks very slowly and carefully sits down.)*
MALCOLM. Are you okay?
WILLIAM. No worse than the day before. What we got?
ENNIS. Well, you and I are having some of Ms. Sharon's classic biscuits and gravy with a side of fried potatoes. But Monsieur Malcolm over there has acquired more sophisticated tastebuds at the university, and is therefore dining upon a turkey bacon and egg white English muffin with a grapefruit.
MALCOLM. I will enjoy my grapefruit and you can enjoy clogged arteries. Pops, do you want some sugar in your coffee?
WILLIAM. You forgot the chocolate milk, didn't you?
MALCOLM. No, I got you a half-gallon. I just thought you'd want some coffee first.
WILLIAM. I can't do coffee like I use to. I get dizzy. But if you bought it for me, I can …

MALCOLM. No, no. That's fine. I'll pour some milk for you.

WILLIAM. But if you bought coffee.

ENNIS. I'll take it. Extra coffee might loosen my clogged arteries. *(Malcolm pours milk and hands it to William.)*

WILLIAM. Thank you. You know your mama was the one that got me drinking that stuff. I wasn't always so crazy about chocolate milk. Sonia was the one that got me hooked. It was our drink. It was our thing.

ENNIS. Okay, so let's name the game. Sevens or nines. *(Ennis dumps dominoes on the table face down and begins shuffling them.)*

MALCOLM. You don't want to eat first.

ENNIS. What? You can't hold your bones and eat a sandwich at the same time? I've been waiting since you left last August to play and I have to wait for you to finish your fancy meal. You done got soft.

MALCOLM. Fine. How many are we pulling?

ENNIS. That's what I'm asking. Sevens or nines?

WILLIAM. I say we play nines. That's what we normally play.

ENNIS. Yeah, you right. Sevens is for rookies. Nines separate the boys from the men. You boys ready to throw some bones? *(All three men sit, eat and play bones.)*

WILLIAM. This is good.

ENNIS. Yeah, nobody does it like Sharon.

WILLIAM. No, I mean … this. Us. *(Beat.)*

ENNIS. So, Pops.

WILLIAM. Yeah.

ENNIS. You ready to tell us why you're wearing an eye patch. I mean, if you're not then …

WILLIAM. Not yet. Let's talk about something else. Let's talk about Malcolm.

MALCOLM. No, you've been talking about me ever since I got back yesterday.

WILLIAM. You have a master's degree. How many people around here can say that?

ENNIS. And working at the EPA. That's pretty sweet, little bruh.

MALCOLM. It's not too hard to get.

ENNIS. I couldn't get it, and I'm a genius. Made up my own science and everything. I forgot to tell you about that, Pops.

WILLIAM. Nowadays any job is a good job.

MALCOLM. You're right, but —

ENNIS. When do you start? Monday?

MALCOLM. Yeah, Monday.

WILLIAM. The EPA. What exactly do they do?

ENNIS. They're the EPA, Pops. They do … a bunch of stuff. They … Malcolm's the one who works there. He'll tell you.

MALCOLM. You know what. I'd rather hear about you, Ennis.

ENNIS. You know all you need to know about me. I'm a skilled domino player, a Gemini, and dead sexy.

MALCOLM. And you have a baby on the way. I want to hear about that.

ENNIS. Oh, hell no. I came by here to get away from all that. Tammy's family is in town, man. All they want to do is talk about the baby. And I'm excited. I really am, but damn. A nigga need a break.

MALCOLM. Ennis.

ENNIS. What? *(Pause.)* Shit. I love black people. I love black people. I love black people. I love black people. I love black people.

MALCOLM. Okay, so we'll wait to talk about the baby. How about work? Is the restaurant …

ENNIS. Whoa, whoa. Another bad topic of conversation.

MALCOLM. Fine. Uhm … Okay. *(Pause.)*

WILLIAM. I had the strangest dream.

MALCOLM. Alright. Tell us about it.

ENNIS. Let me guess what this one was about. Time travel. No, better yet, aliens. Malcolm, last week Pops said he had this dream he was abducted by aliens. But the aliens just wanted directions, right? So Pops gets in the spaceship —

WILLIAM. Actually, I dreamt about your mama. We were in a boat, a small boat, out on the ocean. I think it was before you were born, Malcolm. Because Ennis was there and you weren't. And your mother was alive and there. She was wearing that green dress she bought after we got married. I swear if you saw that dress in a store or on a hanger somewhere it would be the ugliest thing ever. But on your mother it was breathtaking. Anyway, she was wearing that dress, and it was windy so her hair was blowing all over the place. She was holding you, Ennis. You were no more than two years old, maybe. And we were having a great time. We were laughing and sailing, and it was perfect. Until the boat sprung a leak, and started to go down. I was okay because I could swim, but you and your mother couldn't. The boat was really starting to sink and I had to do something quick. I could swim back to shore but not carrying you both. I was going to have to leave one of you.

MALCOLM. What'd you do?

WILLIAM. I woke up. I didn't … I don't know. Maybe I shouldn't have brought that up.

MALCOLM. No, it was good. I'm glad you told us.

ENNIS. Whose play is it?

MALCOLM. What?

ENNIS. Whose play? We're still playing bones, aren't we?

MALCOLM. Yeah, but Pops was telling us about his dream.

ENNIS. I heard. I just thought we were still playing bones.

MALCOLM. We are, but the man is sitting here trying …

WILLIAM. It's fine. I was done talking so … Let's … It's my play. *(Pause.)*

ENNIS. What's the score?

MALCOLM. I have twenty. You and Pops have twenty-five.

ENNIS. Make that forty. *(Ennis puts down a domino.)*

MALCOLM. I'll take fifteen. *(Malcolm puts down a domino.)*

WILLIAM. Things are heating up. *(William puts down a domino.)*

MALCOLM. Whoa, Pops. What's that?

WILLIAM. That's all I could play.

MALCOLM. No, look at the last bone you put down. *(William looks at the domino.)*

WILLIAM. Did I score?

ENNIS. No, you put the wrong bone down. You put a five on a four.

WILLIAM. Where?

ENNIS. Your last play. Right here. *(Ennis points and William struggles to see.)*

WILLIAM. Oh … Well, I guess I lose a turn.

MALCOLM. It's okay. Just play another.

WILLIAM. You sure?

ENNIS. Yeah, it's not like either one of you are going to win.

WILLIAM. Alright. *(Takes his domino back, studies the board, and carefully puts down another.)* I guess I'll take twenty.

MALCOLM. Look out. The old school bringing heat.

ENNIS. Bring it on. I don't fear the heat. Why? Because … *(Slams down a domino.)* Twenty-five! I'm sorry boys, but I can't be touched. And you know this.

MALCOLM. I should have known this is about the time you start talking shit.

ENNIS. Friendly shit-talking is an intricate part of bones. Has it been that long? Have you forgotten this?

MALCOLM. No, I welcome it. Normally when your shit-talking goes up, your domino playing goes down.

ENNIS. Oh, not today. It's looking like I'm going to take this game. And when I smell victory I can't help it. I have to talk about it.

WILLIAM. Whose turn?

ENNIS. It's Malcolm's play. But that last twenty-five I threw out there shook the college boy up a bit. They didn't teach him about this out there. He's spooked.

MALCOLM. I'm concentrating.

ENNIS. Study long, study wrong, little bro. See Pops, I'm in his head. He doesn't know what to do. Well, I'll tell you what to do. Play that five-deuce you've been holding on to. That way, Pops can throw out his six-deuce. I'll lock the game up and get the doubles you've been holding on to. Do that.

WILLIAM. What makes you think he has the five-deuce?

ENNIS. Just watch, Pops. Play that shit, Malcolm. *(Pause.)* Play that shit. *(Pause.)* Don't be scared, play that shit.

MALCOLM. Damn it. *(Malcolm puts down a domino, he has the five-two.)*

ENNIS. I knew it! I knew you had it! Domin-ology!

MALCOLM. What!

ENNIS. Domin-ology. I'm a domin-ologist, baby.

MALCOLM. Earlier you were a broke-ologist, now you're a domin-ologist.

ENNIS. What can I say? You ain't the only one in the house with two degrees.

MALCOLM. Do you hear your son over here? He can't help but talk shit because he's filled with it.

ENNIS. Pops, don't listen to him. Just play that six-deuce like I said. I'll lock it up, and take all the points.

WILLIAM. If that's what you think? *(William plays the six-two.)*

ENNIS. Thank you sir, as I promised … *(Ennis slams a domino.)* The game is locked up. Give me my points.

MALCOLM. You're just going to assume you got the smallest hand?

ENNIS. Well, I know I'm smaller than you with that big five you got. But if we must, then turn them over. *(All turn over their dominoes.)* Damn, Malcolm! I knew you had the big five, but the double four too! Thank you, thank you, and thank you!

MALCOLM. Hold on! I think Pops got you beat. *(All three men*

look at William's dominoes. He has the lowest hand.)
ENNIS. Bullshit!
MALCOLM. Well played, old man, well played.
ENNIS. Malcolm, you still the one giving up the most points.
MALCOLM. I'd much rather give them up to Pops than to you.
WILLIAM. Thank you, son.
MALCOLM. So what's that, Ennis? Pops one, domin-ology zero.
ENNIS. Whatever. Let's keep playing.
MALCOLM. I'm not getting under your skin, am I? Just a little friendly shit-talking. I would've thought a broke-ologist like you would understand.
WILLIAM. I thought he was a domin-ologist.
ENNIS. I'm a nigga that just wants to play dominoes. Come on.
MALCOLM. Ennis …
ENNIS. I love black people. I love black people. I love black people. I love black people. I love black people.
WILLIAM. You love black people?
ENNIS. Don't we all?
MALCOLM. Tammy thinks Ennis uses the N-word too much.
WILLIAM. Which he does.
MALCOLM. And with the baby coming and all, she wants him to start watching what he's saying.
ENNIS. So every time I say, you know what, I have to say "I love black people" five times.
WILLIAM. Is it working?
ENNIS. Nigga, what do you think?
MALCOLM. Ennis!
ENNIS. I'm just playing, I'm just playing. But it's hard. The N-word is like vocabulary cocaine. That shit's addictive. *(Ennis' cell phone rings. He looks at it and cringes.)* Hold on. *(Ennis picks up the phone.)* Hey, baby … I don't know. We just started … We don't need all that. We talked about … Baby, you're not listening … You know what. I'm going to call you right back. Okay. *(Ennis hangs up.)*
MALCOLM. Baby mama drama?
ENNIS. A little bit. If you two would excuse me, I'm going to step outside.
MALCOLM. Don't want us to hear you getting chewed out?
ENNIS. Don't want you to hear a true pimp-ologist in action. It might scare you. Be right back. *(Ennis exits outside.)*
WILLIAM. It doesn't always seem like it, but he and Tammy have

been doing well. I'm proud of him. I'm proud of you, too. I wish I could have been there to see you graduate.

MALCOLM. You were at my high school graduation. You were there when I got my bachelor's. It's all the same. And Ennis said you were having more pain and the doctor thought it would …

WILLIAM. I don't care what any doctor says. You should have had family there.

MALCOLM. I was fine. I'm not worried about that, right now. I'm worried about your eye. *(Pause.)* I got to know, Pops. Did you hurt yourself?

WILLIAM. No, I don't think I did.

MALCOLM. What's wrong?

WILLIAM. It's a little embarrassing.

MALCOLM. Tell me.

WILLIAM. Well, I was taking a nap and when I woke up. My eye was kind of … I don't know. Crossed.

MALCOLM. Crossed. Like how?

WILLIAM. Like crossed. Like … Look. *(William raises the eye patch so that Malcolm can see his eye.)*

MALCOLM. Shit, Pops.

WILLIAM. Just when I think I'm feeling better this happens. *(Ennis enters.)*

ENNIS. I don't understand that girl. We talked about that damn changing table! We can change the baby on the floor, on the couch. And she agreed with me on that until her mother said she needed one. Now we got to run out to the store and get an eighty-dollar changing table.

MALCOLM. Ennis, come look at this.

WILLIAM. He doesn't have to.

MALCOLM. Just let him see.

ENNIS. What am I looking at?

MALCOLM. Show him, Pops. *(William shows Ennis his eye.)*

ENNIS. What the f — ?

WILLIAM. That's why I'm keeping it covered up.

ENNIS. When did that happen?

WILLIAM. Earlier today.

MALCOLM. And you've been taking the medicine?

WILLIAM. Yeah. The pills and the shots.

ENNIS. We've been spending all that money on that expensive-ass medicine and it ain't doing shit.

WILLIAM. This is MS we're talking about here, not a head cold.
ENNIS. I know, but modern medicine has come a long way. Right, Malcolm? We got people cloning sheep, making robotic body parts; they can do damn near anything. But the best they can do for you is give you a bunch of expensive medicine that don't work?
WILLIAM. What do you want? A cure?
ENNIS. Yes. I want a cure.
WILLIAM. So do I.
MALCOLM. So what do we do? Call the doctor?
WILLIAM. No. He told me this could happen, so I'll just keep taking this expensive medicine that don't work.
ENNIS. Well, I'll get it ready for you. *(Ennis gets the medicine and puts it in the syringe.)* After we do this, I'm gonna have to go back over to the house. For some reason Tammy thinks she needs to get that thing right now. So we can finish the game tonight.
MALCOLM. How often do you take that? *(Indicating the syringe.)*
WILLIAM. I take the MS shot once a day, pills for stiffness twice a day.
MALCOLM. And you give him the shot every time?
WILLIAM. I'd do it myself but I can't see the marks on the syringe anymore.
ENNIS. Now that you're back, little bro, I'll show you how to do it. It's pretty easy actually. All you gotta do is make sure there're no bubbles in it and fill it up to the one-ml mark. That simple.
WILLIAM. You can stick my arm or my thigh.
ENNIS. I do the arm, because the thigh is awkward.
WILLIAM. It hurts more, too.
ENNIS. Once you get it down I can just have you give Pops his shots. I won't be able to come over as much once the baby gets here.
MALCOLM. I know.
WILLIAM. When you two get some free time, there's a bunch of old stuff upstairs I need to sort through.
ENNIS. It might take a while to get through all that.
WILLIAM. If we pick one day every week, we can get it done before the end of the year. I want to paint up there, too.
ENNIS. I don't have much time nowadays. I've been working doubles.
WILLIAM. Malcolm can help now that he's back.
ENNIS. Okay. Let's do it on Sundays.
WILLIAM. After we clean we can cook out and watch the game.

ENNIS. That sounds like a plan.

MALCOLM. What if I didn't stay?

ENNIS. What do you mean?

MALCOLM. What if I go back to Connecticut?

ENNIS. I hope you're talking about for a weekend.

MALCOLM. It's something I've been thinking about and I'm not even sure but … I just wonder if it would be better to go back.

ENNIS. Better for who?

MALCOLM. I know I should have said something earlier but I didn't want to kill the mood right away.

WILLIAM. I just thought you were settling in here. You have the job at the EPA.

MALCOLM. I was only going to work there through the summer.

WILLIAM. What's in Connecticut?

MALCOLM. I got another job offer, Pops. I'd be teaching at the university, mostly lower level classes, but I get to work with Professor Coldridge. He's an environmentalist, an activist really. He's been my mentor for the past few years.

ENNIS. Wait a minute. How … You know what, let's just do this medicine. Which arm, Pops?

WILLIAM. Huh?

ENNIS. Which arm, Pops?

WILLIAM. The right one today.

MALCOLM. Look, I don't want you to think I'm …

ENNIS. Shhh. You ready? *(William nods his head. Ennis carefully gives him a shot in the arm. All three men watch intently.)*

WILLIAM. I've been doing this every day for nearly a year now. I've never gotten use to it.

MALCOLM. Damn, Pops.

WILLIAM. I love having you here. Things seem more the way they should be, but I'm here to help you, not hold you back.

MALCOLM. I just wanted you two to know what I was thinking about.

ENNIS. I'm out. I'll be back later on tonight.

MALCOLM. Bro, I don't want you to be …

ENNIS. I'm not. It's just … Tammy's waiting.

MALCOLM. So we're good?

ENNIS. Yeah. We're good. *(Ennis exits.)*

WILLIAM. He'll be fine. *(Malcolm begins cleaning up breakfast as William starts putting up the dominoes. But William thinks about it and leaves them out. Lights down. Lights up. It is later that evening. Malcolm stands by the window looking out onto the neighborhood. William enters from upstairs with the patch still over his eye.)* I thought Ennis would've been back by now.

MALCOLM. Maybe he's not coming.

WILLIAM. No, I'm sure Tammy just has him running all over town, doing a ton of things before the baby gets here. You know she's due any minute. It's going to be an exciting summer.

MALCOLM. Pops, when was old man Calvin's house torn down?

WILLIAM. Oh, that was a shame. He died this past November, and the house was gone a few months after that.

MALCOLM. And now it's an empty lot filled with trash and weeds. I would go over there right now with a Weed Eater and some trash bags, but I'm afraid I'd get lost in there. I love this neighborhood, but I have a hard time looking at it.

WILLIAM. Every neighborhood has its ugly. I try not to focus on those parts.

MALCOLM. What happened to the restaurants and the grocery stores and the nice apartments?

WILLIAM. It's not all about the buildings, son. It's the people in them. Don't forget the people here.

MALCOLM. You're right. But, I don't connect with them like I used to. This morning when Ennis and I were at Sharon's getting breakfast, I saw Kevin Jones.

WILLIAM. Oh yeah. I liked that kid. Big musclehead, though.

MALCOLM. I know, we called him Bobblehead Jones, but that was my boy. We were tight, Pops.

WILLIAM. I remember.

MALCOLM. When I saw him this morning, it felt like we were speaking different languages. It's just not the same. I've been away, he's been here. I've got two degrees, he's got two kids. I'm worried about our economy and global warming. He's worried about the police and how he's going to pay the electric bill. What are we going to talk about?

WILLIAM. But Malcolm, you've always been different from those kids you use to play ball with. You and your brother. It's harder to see in him but it's there. You just have a few more things to figure out.

MALCOLM. Exactly. That's the only reason I'd go back to Connecticut. Not to get away from you guys, but to move towards something. There's a big movement going on and I want to establish myself in it. I know I could work at the EPA, but I'd rather do something I'm passionate about. At UConn I would teach class during the week and on weekends myself, Professor Coldridge, and a group of other people go out to poor neighborhoods. Neighborhoods just like this one. We educate people on how to grow their own food, teach them how to keep the town clean. All I need is a few more years. After I learn exactly how to rebuild a community, I'll come back and make something happen around here.

WILLIAM. You don't have to explain it to me. You do what you think is best.

MALCOLM. I want to be here for you, Pops, I do.

WILLIAM. Don't you worry about me. Go, if you need to. I'll be fine. You remind me of somebody when you get like that.

MALCOLM. Yeah?

WILLIAM. Yeah, you get this spirit in you. This look on your face. Everybody always said that you and your brother were just like me, but I can see the Sonia in you. She's there. Always has been.

MALCOLM. I remember her pancakes.

WILLIAM. Oh yeah.

MALCOLM. I swear, every morning I'd wake up to the smell of those pancakes. Sometimes she'd put fresh fruit in them. Apples, bananas, blueberries, whatever she had in the refrigerator.

WILLIAM. And once in a while chocolate chips.

MALCOLM. That's right. Chocolate chips with powdered sugar on top. I remember that. I remember that smell for some reason. And it's weird because sometimes I can't remember her face. Not perfectly, not detailed like I want. I remember the smell of pancakes more than what Mama's face looked like. I don't know how to feel about that. It's like I lose a little of her here and there as time goes by.

WILLIAM. I understand.

MALCOLM. I do remember that green dress, though. I had almost forgotten it until you brought it up this morning when you were talking about your dream.

WILLIAM. God, she was beautiful in it. Perfect. *(Pause.)* Thank you for talking about your mama. It ain't always easy.

MALCOLM. I don't mind it. At all.

WILLIAM. Your brother does. I bring her up and he gets quiet.

MALCOLM. Ennis just deals with things differently. Sometimes he can't stop running his mouth, other times he keeps it all in.

WILLIAM. I think it might be me.

MALCOLM. Don't start blaming yourself, Pops.

WILLIAM. I'm not blaming myself. I'm saying that he's been here with me as I've gotten worse. And watching someone … you know.

MALCOLM. I know. *(Ennis enters from outside. He's been drinking a little.)*

ENNIS. One hundred and eighty-seven damn dollars! Can you believe that?

WILLIAM. You've been gone for a while.

ENNIS. Blame Tammy, man. Had me running all over town buying up a ton of shit. One hundred and eighty-seven dollars worth of shit we don't need.

WILLIAM. Babies are expensive, son.

ENNIS. I know, Pops.

WILLIAM. That's why you picked up extra shifts. You're saving money.

ENNIS. Exactly, so how in the hell am I supposed to save money when Tammy got me spending it all? You know what I'm saying. And what the fuck is a Baby Bjorn?

MALCOLM. I have no idea.

ENNIS. Neither do I, but I had to buy that, some funny-looking blankets with flaps, more damn baby clothes, and diapers. Thirty dollars in diapers alone.

WILLIAM. You'll be doing that once a week.

ENNIS. I can't. That's too much. Thirty dollars a week just so the kid can piss and shit. There's gotta be another way. Malcolm, you're into science. You know about all the things they can do with genes. Somebody has to be able to genetically alter a baby so it doesn't poop. Make me a poopless baby.

MALCOLM. How much did you spend on the changing table?

ENNIS. What?

MALCOLM. Changing table. That's what you left to get in the first place.

ENNIS. Never even looked at one. The whole time we were out. So I still have to get that.

WILLIAM. Well, now that you're back we can finish the game from earlier. I kept the bones right where we left them.

ENNIS. Not now. I got a better idea. We need to take a road trip.

WILLIAM. Have you been drinking?

ENNIS. I may have stopped by a bar. I may have had a few drinks with some friends. I may even be a bit tipsy.

WILLIAM. You drove here drunk.

ENNIS. Tipsy. I drove here a bit tipsy.

WILLIAM. And then you're going to drive back drunk.

ENNIS. Tipsy, Pops. And no. I'll crash here tonight.

WILLIAM. There you go again.

ENNIS. There I go again with what? Every time ... Forget about it. I didn't come back here to talk about me. I came here to tell you about this road trip I think we should go on.

MALCOLM. Can we discuss what I brought up earlier instead?

ENNIS. About you going to Connecticut?

MALCOLM. Yes.

ENNIS. I said that we were good.

MALCOLM. I don't think we really are.

ENNIS. Okay, maybe we're not, but that's what this road trip is about. It's going to put things into perspective.

MALCOLM. No, Ennis. You're avoiding this. We don't have time to wait around on a road trip.

ENNIS. That's the thing. We don't have to wait. We can go tonight.

WILLIAM. And you think you're in the right condition to drive.

ENNIS. Actually I was going to let you drive, Pops. I want to see the cops' face when they pull over the black pirate.

MALCOLM. Ennis.

ENNIS. Malcolm can drive.

MALCOLM. I'm not driving anywhere tonight.

ENNIS. Fuck it. We don't have to drive. It's right down the street.

MALCOLM. Where are you trying to take us?

ENNIS. I wanted it to surprise you, but if you must know ... *(Ennis jumps on the coffee table or couch.)* I've been inspired by Pops' eye patch. I say we go treasure hunting tonight. Arrr.

MALCOLM. And what kind of treasure are we gonna find around in this neighborhood? A pot of gold teeth?

ENNIS. Come on, matey. We'll take a quick journey down the street to find our booty. I know you like booty.

MALCOLM. Any booty that can be found down the street, I want nothing to do with. *(Ennis jumps down.)*

ENNIS. Look, I just want to take you down the street and across the bridge to the old John Brown statue. Remember that?

MALCOLM. That thing is still up?

ENNIS. Yes, it is. Pops told us that John Brown himself hid his treasure somewhere out there and no one ever found it.

MALCOLM. We used to dig there for hours. We broke, like, ten plastic shovels.

WILLIAM. The city's been trying to get rid of that area. They want to clear it all out and build some factory over there.

ENNIS. That's why we should go now. Before it's gone.

MALCOLM. Wait, no one is getting rid of a historical landmark. The underground railroad passed through there. Hell, isn't that where Great-Grandma is buried?

WILLIAM. And your great-grandpa.

ENNIS. Let's go pay them a visit. Maybe they know where the treasure is.

WILLIAM. Son, you know I made up the whole thing about …

ENNIS. Ah, ah, ah. Don't you do it. Don't you ruin the magic for me. Tonight we're going to do what we never did as kids. We're going to find that treasure.

WILLIAM. It's getting too late for me to be roaming around outside.

ENNIS. Well, you can stay here. I really just need Malcolm.

MALCOLM. And we'll be right back?

ENNIS. Oh yeah.

MALCOLM. Fine. Let's go.

WILLIAM. What about the domino game?

ENNIS. We'll play when we get back. Okay.

MALCOLM. Are we hitting the street or taking the short cut?

ENNIS. Short cut. I don't feel like fooling with them niggas off of Twenty-second.

MALCOLM. Ennis.

ENNIS. Oh, I love black people, I love black people, blah, blah, blah, whatever. Let's go. *(Malcolm and Ennis exit outside. William goes to the window and watches his sons for a while. Then he goes to the kitchen and opens up the refrigerator. He is having problems seeing what's inside. He finally pulls out a container of orange juice. He puts it up to his face and sees that it's not what he wanted. He puts it back and looks again. Sonia enters from upstairs. She sees William struggling to find something.)*

SONIA. Looking for something?

WILLIAM. What?

SONIA. You know I keep it on the bottom. It freezes if you put it on the top shelf.

WILLIAM. My God. Baby doll.

SONIA. Don't you "baby doll" me. You were supposed to buy me a new refrigerator last year. I don't mind doing without, but if this refrigerator up and stops running, then what are you going to do?

WILLIAM. I'm sorry, baby.

SONIA. I'm sorry, too. *(Pause.)* Now, move on out the way. I'll get the chocolate milk and pour us both a glass. *(Sonia pours two glasses of chocolate milk.)*

WILLIAM. Sonia, I can't believe it.

SONIA. Believe what. This ain't the first glass of milk I've poured for you.

WILLIAM. You're here, right here with me, and we're together.

SONIA. Yeah, we are. And I don't plan on going anywhere.

WILLIAM. That's good to hear. I love you, baby.

SONIA. I love you, too.

WILLIAM. Baby, first thing in the morning I'm going out to buy you that refrigerator.

SONIA. Now, William —

WILLIAM. No, you're right. I should have bought it years ago. And there's a sale going on down at Sears.

SONIA. We both know we don't have the money for that right now. I just want us to make it a priority. The minute we do have the money that's what we should do.

WILLIAM. Sonia, you're always going without and that ain't fair. I know we're broke but I can do something for you.

SONIA. Broke? No, the year before we got married we were broke. We were living in Lawrence. Do you remember that?

WILLIAM. I tried to forget. We didn't have a damn thing.

SONIA. Not even an apartment for a while. We lived with Vanessa for a few months in that little bitty basement.

WILLIAM. That's right. That little-ass, hot-ass basement.

SONIA. It was in the middle of the summer.

WILLIAM. We would lay down there on that old raggedy mattress I found somewhere. We lied down there, hot as hell. Sweating like two runaway slaves.

SONIA. And all those roaches.

WILLIAM. Good God. Your friend Vanessa had some serious roaches.

SONIA. Bold too. Most roaches run when you turn on the lights. It was like these damn things put on sunglasses and kept going.

WILLIAM. I didn't even want to step on them at first. I figured Vanessa didn't care so maybe she wanted them around. Maybe they were her pets.

SONIA. I was so glad you got that job at Randy's and we could move into this house. I know this place wasn't much to look at, but it was ours.

WILLIAM. It was also supposed to be temporary.

SONIA. It's taken care of us over the years. No, it's not in the ideal neighborhood, but it's nothing to be ashamed of. You built that fence around the yard, we painted a few times. We worked with what we had.

WILLIAM. We said no more than five years. That's what we agreed on. That way Malcolm and Ennis could have been in a different school district. I never liked this one.

SONIA. They did fine. Our boys are bright, very bright. And getting so big. It seems like they were babies and now look at them. Malcolm reminds me of you so much.

WILLIAM. I was just telling him how much he reminds me of you.

SONIA. Oh, William. I feel like doing something tonight.

WILLIAM. Doing what?

SONIA. I don't care. I just don't want to be cooped up in this house all day.

WILLIAM. You want to go out to eat?

SONIA. We have food here. I want to do something … I don't know. Something else.

WILLIAM. Well, we can look in the newspaper and see what's going on.

SONIA. No, no. I want to dance. Let's go dancing.

WILLIAM. Dancing?

SONIA. Yes.

WILLIAM. I can't dance.

SONIA. I know that. You're not good at all. But it's cute. And it never stopped you before. Come on. Take me dancing.

WILLIAM. Maybe go down to the Blue Room, show those young bucks how it's done.

SONIA. We should clean up a little bit. Try to look nice. I'll put on that bracelet, maybe change into that cute red dress.

WILLIAM. No, don't change dresses. I'm in love with this one.

SONIA. I've been wearing this all day and I want to look nice.

WILLIAM. You look great.

SONIA. Not good enough to go out. You too, William. Put on

that nice white shirt and even a tie. Oh, and you need to shave.

WILLIAM. It ain't that bad.

SONIA. We can't be dancing cheek to cheek with that steel wool on your face.

WILLIAM. All right. I'll shave.

SONIA. Good.

WILLIAM. And put on my brown tie.

SONIA. That tie won't match either one of my dresses.

WILLIAM. Then we'll buy you a new one.

SONIA. Don't be crazy. You know we don't have the money.

WILLIAM. We can figure it out.

SONIA. Or I can wear what I have.

WILLIAM. When was the last time you bought a new outfit?

SONIA. I don't know. I was …

WILLIAM. Wouldn't you like something new?

SONIA. Yes, but …

WILLIAM. Let me do this for you, baby.

SONIA. We should wait.

WILLIAM. Let me make you happy.

SONIA. William.

WILLIAM. That's all I ever wanted to do, was to make you happy.

SONIA. You can't make me happy, William. Not all the time. You just can't. And it's not your fault. I love you but this is not the life I dreamed I'd be living. I was going to finish my degree. I wanted to move downtown to the artsy district, paint portraits that spoke of my inner-city pain. Sell them for three hundred bucks apiece. Instead I'm stuck in the house all day with two rowdy boys watching life zoom past me. This is not where I thought we'd end up. You're right. We said no more than five years, and look. We're still here. The same house. The same damn neighborhood. And you and I … us. We don't talk anymore, not like we use to. I'm lonely. So yes, there are times I am very unhappy. And there's nothing you or a brand-new dress can do about it. You're my husband. You're not solely responsible for my happiness. I know that one day we'll both be as happy as we dreamed we'd be the first day we met, but that's going to take a little more time. Until then, just love me like you always have. Okay. Love me and take me dancing.

WILLIAM. I do love you.

SONIA. Good. Now let's get ready. I want to get there before it gets too crowded. *(Sonia grabs William's arm to lead him upstairs.)*

WILLIAM. Oh, I almost forgot.

SONIA. What?

WILLIAM. It's my … I don't know if I should go out. *(William starts to raise the eye patch to show Sonia his eye. Sonia grabs his hand and stops him.)*

SONIA. I don't care. I just want to be with you. *(Sonia and William exit upstairs hand in hand. Malcolm and Ennis enter from outside. They are carrying a very large black garden gnome. His name is Stubby. They speak in pirate accents.)*

ENNIS. Ahoy, matey. Land ho.

MALCOLM. Arr, the sweet smell of home. Feels mighty good to be back. *(They sit Stubby down. Malcolm kneels and kisses the floor.)*

ENNIS. And even more importantly, we returned with a treasure.

MALCOLM. We should tell the captain of our discovery.

ENNIS. Aye, call old Blackbeard down to have a look. *(Calling upstairs.)*

MALCOLM. Hey, captain! *(William doesn't answer.)* Captain! *(Still no answer from William.)* He must be asleep.

ENNIS. Oh, well. The treasure is all ours.

MALCOLM. And what a treasure he is. We cash in Old Stubby here for at least a thousand gold pieces.

ENNIS. Ne'er. *(Both breaking accents again.)*

MALCOLM. Ennis.

ENNIS. What?

MALCOLM. Didn't you just say … You know.

ENNIS. No, no. Like never without the "v."

MALCOLM. Oh, ne'er.

ENNIS. Yeah, I don't even know if pirates said that. *(Back to the pirate accents.)* Like I was saying. Never! Me dear mate Stubby is far too valuable to sell away.

MALCOLM. I suppose you're right. The little landlubber is as cute as a shipmate after a bottle of rum. What do you suggest we be doing with his chubby dark soul?

ENNIS. Keep him around for a while. See if the little niglet brings us any good luck.

MALCOLM. Sounds like a mighty fine idea. Welcome aboard, Stubby. *(Malcolm extends his hand out for Stubby to shake. Stubby doesn't shake. Malcolm pats him on the face instead.)*

ENNIS. Now Stubby, if you're gonna stick around …

MALCOLM. Wait one minute. I believe we have an imposter

among us. Look. *(Malcolm shows Ennis his hand. It has a little brown paint on it from Stubby's face.)*

ENNIS. Well, I'll be. *(Ennis touches Stubby face and also rubs off a little paint.)*

MALCOLM. I should have known. He's painted.

ENNIS. In-cog-negro if you will.

MALCOLM. You're gonna pay for this, Stubby. *(Ennis jumps upon the coffee table or couch.)*

ENNIS. I say, to the plank! Arr. *(Malcolm dropping the accent.)*

MALCOLM. Bro, what are we doing?

ENNIS. We're gonna make old Stubby here walk the plank.

MALCOLM. No, seriously. What is this? *(Ennis drops the accent.)*

ENNIS. We're playing around like we use to. Playing like we're pirates.

MALCOLM. I know that. But why?

ENNIS. Because it's fun, Malcolm. Can we not have fun?

MALCOLM. We stole Ms. Moore's garden gnome right out of her yard.

ENNIS. I know. I've always hated this creepy-looking thing.

MALCOLM. We're not keeping this, are we?

ENNIS. Her old ass will never know it's missing.

MALCOLM. Where in the hell are we going to put this?

ENNIS. He'll go well with the bathroom.

MALCOLM. There's no way. Stubby can't stand there watching me pee.

ENNIS. I'm just kidding. We'll take him back tomorrow.

MALCOLM. Good.

ENNIS. But this was exciting. Felt like old times, right?

MALCOLM. It was fun. I still don't understand why we went but it was fun.

ENNIS. You don't understand why we went?

MALCOLM. You told me before we left that this trip was going to have something to do with me leaving. That's what I wanted to talk about.

ENNIS. I thought our little hunt would change your mind on some things. We haven't had fun like that in a long time. Hell, this house hasn't felt like this for a long time. You see how happy Pops is. We can't have it like this if you're hundreds of miles away.

MALCOLM. If you and Pops were the only factors I had to consider, you know I'd stay. But there's so much more.

ENNIS. Like what?

MALCOLM. Like … It's just a lot. A lot of reasons to stay. A lot of reasons to go.

ENNIS. A woman?

MALCOLM. A who?

ENNIS. A woman. Did you fall in love out there?

MALCOLM. No, why would you assume that?

ENNIS. Just trying to figure out why you want to leave.

MALCOLM. I told you. It's complicated.

ENNIS. Well, let's break it all down. *(Ennis looks for a notebook and a pen.)*

MALCOLM. What are you doing?

ENNIS. Looking for paper and something to write with.

MALCOLM. Why?

ENNIS. Like I said, we're going to break it down. Make a list of all the reasons why you should go and all the reasons why you should stay.

MALCOLM. I think this is something that I have to figure for myself, Ennis.

ENNIS. But this decision doesn't just affect you, Malcolm. So you're going to have to humor me. *(Ennis hands Malcolm the notebook and a pen.)*

MALCOLM. You can't write now?

ENNIS. You know my handwriting looks like shit, and I'm still a little drunk.

MALCOLM. I thought you were tipsy.

ENNIS. Whatever. I'll start. Reasons why you should stay. First reason, barbeque.

MALCOLM. I should stay in K.C. for barbeque?

ENNIS. It's not the strongest reason, but it's true. You know as well as I do that they can't grill out there like we do it in the Midwest. The chicken, the K.C. strip, rib tips.

MALCOLM. I have missed some rib tips. But you know what I haven't missed? Crackheads.

ENNIS. There's crackheads everywhere. Kansas City, Connecticut, I'll bet Disneyland got crackheads.

MALCOLM. Yeah, but they were different where I was. They were functional crackheads. They would smoke crack, go to work, and you wouldn't even know. Crackheads here are obvious.

ENNIS. Alright, I'll let you have it. There may not be a lot of crackheads, but I'm sure there are too many white folks.

MALCOLM. What? That's not true. How would you know?

ENNIS. Just listen to it. "Connecticut." Sounds like a place that's filled to the brim with white folks.

MALCOLM. You live in Kansas. Kansas probably has more white people than anybody.

ENNIS. We live in Kansas City. It's a real city with color in it. There's a difference.

MALCOLM. No, it's Kansas City, Kansas. Why do you care anyway? Tammy's white.

ENNIS. She's Greek. Her great-grandfather was Greek.

MALCOLM. She looks white to me. And there's nothing wrong with that.

ENNIS. I know. But it might be nice to live somewhere you don't stick out so much. Alright. Where are we at? Two to one, you stay?

MALCOLM. Let's not forget the job at UConn. We're tied at two.

ENNIS. But you have a job here. A good job.

MALCOLM. It's not what I really want to do.

ENNIS. You think I really want to work at that damn restaurant? You think I want to spend the rest of my life dishing out potato salad and coming home smelling like charred meat?

MALCOLM. I know you don't.

ENNIS. All the things I want to do have taken the back burner to the things I have to do. Which brings me to the fact that you have a nephew on the way.

MALCOLM. I know this.

ENNIS. Tammy's got all sisters in her family. That means you're going to be the kid's only uncle. And he's going to need strong male influences in his life.

MALCOLM. Can you make me feel any worse?

ENNIS. Yes. I was thinking about asking you to be his godfather, but you probably knew that, though.

MALCOLM. Ennis, you're killing me.

ENNIS. The baby will come. You'll barely have time to spend with him before you leave. You'll be away while he grows, when he takes his first steps, when he says "domino."

MALCOLM. Okay, okay. I get the point. But what happens if I stay and never leave? Plan to stay for two years and two years turns into three years. Three years turn to five. Five years turns into ten.

ENNIS. Sure you're not just running away?

MALCOLM. From what?

ENNIS. Pops.

MALCOLM. No. I want to be as close to him as I can, but me being here is not going to cure him.

ENNIS. But it makes him happy. It helps me. I can't keep taking care of him like I do.

MALCOLM. "Taking care of him." He's not helpless.

ENNIS. But he's in bad shape. I don't know how bad, because I'm not a doctor. Not like they know anything. Did you hear him this morning? That weird-ass dream with me and him and Mama in a sinking boat. He's got to save one of us. What in the hell was that?

MALCOLM. I liked it.

ENNIS. Every other day he tells me about some crazy dream he had. He's getting weaker. The whole damn thing with his eye. And it's only going to get worse.

MALCOLM. This family needs money and I get paid well in Connecticut.

ENNIS. I don't care about money. This family needs you.

MALCOLM. I'm not … I don't know. I just … I want to go.

ENNIS. And we need you here. *(Pause.)*

MALCOLM. I think I'm done.

ENNIS. I'm sure I can come up with a few more.

MALCOLM. I'm done, for now.

ENNIS. Okay, what was the final score?

MALCOLM. I lost count.

ENNIS. I bet you did.

MALCOLM. What time do you work in the morning?

ENNIS. Early as hell as always. Why?

MALCOLM. It's starting to get late. That's all.

ENNIS. Is this your subtle way of telling me to go home?

MALCOLM. No, I thought you were staying here anyway.

ENNIS. I don't know. I'm starting to sober up. If I stay here tonight, I'll have to hear Tammy's mouth in the morning. Nag, nag, bitch, bitch, nag, bitch, bitch. That's all I hear nowadays.

MALCOLM. It ain't that bad, is it?

ENNIS. Shit.

MALCOLM. She's just stressed about the baby. I know you probably are too, but … I don't know. Tammy's good for you. I like her.

ENNIS. She's all yours then. I'll take my ass to Connecticut. *(They both laugh.)*

MALCOLM. You were right about one thing.

ENNIS. I'm right about a lot of things, but which particular one are you talking about now?

MALCOLM. There's a woman.

ENNIS. What?

MALCOLM. She's not why I want to go back and I'm not in love. But I did meet someone.

ENNIS. A real girl?

MALCOLM. She is since the operation. *(Pause.)* I'm just messing around with you. Of course it's a real girl. Woman. If you will.

ENNIS. That's fine. It's just that to my knowledge you haven't had a lot of experience with the ladies.

MALCOLM. To your knowledge.

ENNIS. Excuse me.

MALCOLM. I'm picky. But just because I don't tell you everything, doesn't mean there's nothing to be told.

ENNIS. Well. Let's hear the details.

MALCOLM. I'm afraid I can't do that.

ENNIS. Oh, come off this "a gentlemen never tells" bullshit. I'm your brother.

MALCOLM. No, I really can't say anything, because there's not much to say. We're not officially together.

ENNIS. So you two are friends.

MALCOLM. I wouldn't say that either. We messed around a little, but I guess we're just taking our time.

ENNIS. So you and this girl. What's her name?

MALCOLM. Brittany.

ENNIS. You and Brittany … Wait a minute. Is she white?

MALCOLM. Here we go with this again.

ENNIS. I'm just asking. I ain't ever met a sister named Brittany.

MALCOLM. She's black. Just like the thousands of other black people that reside in the state of Connecticut.

ENNIS. Okay. So you and black Brittany aren't dating. What else about her?

MALCOLM. Well, she's a real sweet girl. Real smart. I met her in school. We had chemistry together. Funny, huh. *(Ennis doesn't think it's funny.)* Anyway, she's got a little attitude on her, but not too much. And she's gorgeous. Dark skin, pretty brown eyes, great figure.

ENNIS. She got a fat ass?

MALCOLM. You see, that's why I can't talk to you.

ENNIS. What did I say?

MALCOLM. What do you think you said? "She got a fat ass?"

ENNIS. I was just curious.

MALCOLM. I'm trying to tell you about this woman, a woman that I'm real close to. And all you can think about is … *(William enters from upstairs, carrying a straight-blade razor. He has cut himself shaving. He is dressed up for going out. His nice white shirt is blood-stained. One side of his face is very bloody. One of the cuts is deep.)*

WILLIAM. You boys seen my other razor?

MALCOLM. Shit, Pops.

ENNIS. What in the hell happened?

WILLIAM. Oh, it's not that bad.

ENNIS. Pops, you're bleeding all over the place.

WILLIAM. I couldn't find my new razor, so I had to use the old one.

MALCOLM. I'll get something to clean that up. *(Ennis carefully takes the razor from William. Malcolm looks around the house for bandages and towels.)*

WILLIAM. I don't think it's that bad and we got places to be.

ENNIS. We ain't going anywhere except for maybe the hospital.

MALCOLM. Do we have any bandages?

ENNIS. In the bathroom. *(Malcolm hands Ennis a towel.)*

MALCOLM. Put some pressure on it. *(Malcolm exits to the bathroom as Ennis applies pressure to William's face.)*

WILLIAM. We really need to get going. *(William tries to stand up. Ennis makes him sit.)*

ENNIS. Pops, have you lost your mind? Sit down.

WILLIAM. I've got to finish getting ready.

ENNIS. You've got blood dripping down your face. Sit down!

WILLIAM. She's waiting on me.

ENNIS. What are you talking about? Who? *(Malcolm reenters.)*

MALCOLM. How bad is it?

ENNIS. I don't know yet.

MALCOLM. Let me see. *(Malcolm takes a look at his father's face.)* This is pretty deep, man.

ENNIS. What made you think you had to shave at this time of night?

WILLIAM. I told you we were going out tonight.

ENNIS. We went out. Me and Malcolm just got back.

WILLIAM. I'm not talking about you.

ENNIS. Then who are you talking about?

WILLIAM.   Your mama. Me and your mama were going out tonight. She wanted me to take her dancing.

MALCOLM.   Mama's not here, Pops.

WILLIAM.   Yeah, she was. She was upstairs with me. She told me to shave and I started shaving, and then she came down here for something.

MALCOLM.   No. Mama's not here. She's gone.

WILLIAM.   She leave without me?

ENNIS.   She's dead, Pops. She couldn't have been here. She's been dead for fifteen years.

WILLIAM.   I know, but she was here. I saw her. I touched her. We drank chocolate milk together. *(Malcolm is still looking at William's face.)*

MALCOLM.   Yeah, we might have to go to the hospital. He's going to have to get stitched up.

WILLIAM.   I know she's around here.

ENNIS.   Pops, you got to settle down.

WILLIAM.   But, your mama was …

ENNIS.   No. I don't know what you saw but it wasn't her.

MALCOLM.   We'll take you to the hospital. Everything will be okay after that.

WILLIAM.   I'm sorry.

ENNIS.   Don't be sorry. *(Ennis helps William to his feet.)* Let's just go. Malcolm, can you drive?

MALCOLM.   I got it.

WILLIAM.   I'm sorry.

ENNIS.   It's okay. We'll take care of you.

WILLIAM.   I'm sorry. I'm so sorry.

ENNIS.   Don't worry about it, Pops. We're going to be fine.

MALCOLM.   Careful. Watch your step.

ENNIS.   I got him. You get the car door.

WILLIAM.   I'm sorry. I'm sorry. *(William and Ennis exit outside. Malcolm goes to the kitchen. He looks around for the keys. He finds them on the table. Before he walks off, he sees the two half-drunk glasses of chocolate milk. He just looks at them. He snaps out of it, and exits outside.)*

End of Act One

ACT TWO

Beginning of Act Two. Lights up on the King household. It is mid-August. The dominoes from the game played earlier in the summer are still on the table. Stubby still sits in the living room. William enters from upstairs. He is still wearing the eye patch. He moves a lot slower and his muscles are sore. He is carrying an old box filled with random items.

WILLIAM. You boys home? *(No one answers.)* This is the stuff I was talking about. I thought maybe you could … *(William realizes that his sons are not there.)* I guess it's just me. *(William sees Stubby.)* And you. I thought you'd be gone by now. Ms. Moore has been calling over here all summer asking me about you. *(William gingerly sits down on the couch with the box in front of him.)* I just lie, telling her I don't know anything. And the whole time you're right here. You might as well help me sort through this. Just some old stuff I found. I should have gone through all that junk up there a while ago. *(William thinks for a minute.)* Let's just see what we have in here. *(William reaches into the box and pulls out two ornaments. He's having trouble seeing what they are. His eyesight has gotten worse.)* These better not be what I think they are. *(William looks closer. They are what he thinks they are.)* I'll be damned. I thought I threw all these things away. You see, these aren't the ornaments I originally bought. The ones I bought looked the same, but they weren't the right color. For some reason Sonia wanted the black figurines instead of white. So she took the ones I bought, and exchanged them for these. I come home from work to see these little black people hanging on the Christmas tree. I know she meant well, but little black folks hanging on our tree. It looked like a Klu Klux Christmas. Freaked me out. I didn't think we still had them. *(Sets the ornaments to the side and pulls out a sheet of paper.)* Now this might be a problem. *(William can't make out what's on the paper.)* This is why I wanted the boys to help me. I can't see what this is. *(William looks more but can't make it out.)* Well, I'll wait until they get back. Unless you can make it out. *(Hands the paper to Stubby. Stubby does not take it.)* Thanks for trying … Hey, what's your name? I never asked. *(Stubby, as usual, is silent.)* My name is William. You look like a … Bobby. No, Chauncey. I think your name is Chauncey. That sounds about right? But if you don't like it, just let me know. *(Stubby doesn't answer.)* Well then, Chauncey, let's see what else we have in here. *(William continues searching through the box. He starts pulling out T-shirts.)* This is what I was looking for. *(They are the T-shirts that Sonia made for the family. Four T-shirts, each with one letter on it. The shirts spell out "KING.")* Oh yeah, I don't need to see to know what these are. Sonia made these. She was a pretty good little artist. I wish she could have done more with it. We didn't get to wear the shirts too often because the boys grew up so fast. When we did wear them we looked good. They looked better than anything you could've bought at the store. Ennis and Tammy might want to use them. Whatcha think? *(Stubby is silent.)* You don't say much, do you? *(William continues looking through the box. He pulls out an old cassette tape.)* Ah man! Now, we're talking. You know what this is, Chauncey? This is what they call old school. You wouldn't know nothing about this. This is a tape I made for Sonia when she was stuck at the house with the boys. This here, has a collection of classic cuts. I'm talking about the good shit. *(William gets up slowly and walks over and puts the tape in the radio.)* The boys are always listening to that hip-hop, but since it's just me and you; we're going to do it right this afternoon. This tape has a few Stevie Wonder, some Chaka Khan, a little Smokey Robinson. But if my memory serves me. This tape starts out with the one and only Temptations. *(William puts the tape in and presses play. Something like a slow Temptations song begins.*)* Oh yeah! I told you! This was one of me and Sonia's favorites. *(Sonia comes halfway down the steps and watches William.)* Now this is what we're going to do, Chauncey. I'm going to take this first part. I want you to join me halfway in, with the high part. You look like a bit of a tenor. Then we'll take the chorus together. That's how me and Sonia used to do it. Here it comes. *(William sings the song loudly standing next to Stubby, doing classic Motown dance moves. Stubby decides not to sing or dance. William is filled with energy; almost for a moment he is not sick. Sonia watches on with a smile. Then, to Stubby.)* Okay, Chauncey. This is where you come in. *(He sings. Then, to Stubby.)* This is the real high part. *(Sings. Then, to Stubby.)* Here it is, Chauncey. The

---

* See Special Note on Songs and Recordings on copyright page.

chorus. Don't be afraid to just belt it out. *(Sings. Malcolm and Ennis enter while William continues to groove. Malcolm and Ennis watch, mostly amused but also slightly weirded out. William continues singing and dancing until he sees his two sons watching him.)* Hey, you two are back. We were looking through this old box and found this tape.

MALCOLM. I can't hear you, Pops. The music is too loud.

WILLIAM. Y'all wouldn't know nothing about this music here, but I found some other things you might be interested in.

MALCOLM. Pops, we can't … *(Malcolm goes to turn down the music. Sonia disappears back up the stairs.)* Now, what's going on in here?

ENNIS. We leave the house and you throw a one-man dance party.

WILLIAM. We don't have to stop. We need two more to complete the quartet.

ENNIS. We?

WILLIAM. Yeah, we.

MALCOLM. Are you talking about Mama again?

WILLIAM. No, not this time. I'm talking about my friend Chauncey here. *(William pats Stubby on the head.)*

ENNIS. His name is Stubby.

WILLIAM. Looks like a Chauncey to me.

MALCOLM. Either way, why were you and Chauncey in here Soul-Training it up?

ENNIS. It was a little crazy.

WILLIAM. No more crazy than stealing it from Ms. Moore's front yard. *(Malcolm and Ennis look at each other.)*

MALCOLM. Yeah, Ennis was supposed to return that a while ago.

ENNIS. We were supposed to return that a while ago.

MALCOLM. Well, you never came by when you said you were and I'm not going to carry that damn thing all the way down there by myself.

ENNIS. I have a baby, Malcolm. Did you forget that shit? I can't just come …

WILLIAM. Hey, hey, hey. It's alright. I kind of like the little guy. We had a good time today.

MALCOLM. Well, don't exhaust yourself. Remember the doctor said to take it slow.

WILLIAM. Hey, I know. *(Ennis' cell phone rings. He silences it then gives it a look.)*

MALCOLM. You hungry? I can make you something.

WILLIAM. I can do it.

MALCOLM. We just got done talking about you taking it slow.

WILLIAM. It's just lunch. Not construction work.

MALCOLM. But why not just save your energy and let me take care of it?

WILLIAM. Because I'm tired of feeling helpless. And today is different. Today I feel good. Let me try.

MALCOLM. If you start to wear yourself out, you're taking a break.

WILLIAM. Yes sir. *(William goes to the kitchen to fix lunch. Ennis is still checking his cell phone, looks irritated.)* You two want something?

MALCOLM. Ennis and I ate while we were out.

WILLIAM. Where did you guys go today?

MALCOLM. We just had some errands to run. Stuff we need to take care of before the summer's over.

WILLIAM. Well, hope you took care of them.

ENNIS. Not really.

WILLIAM. Is everything alright?

ENNIS. No, actually. It's a fucked-up world, Pops. It's true, it's just a fucked-up world. But in your current state you probably know that. *(William tries to reach a pot; instead several pots come crashing down. Malcolm rushes over.)*

WILLIAM. No, no. Just an accident. I did things like this before I got sick.

ENNIS. *(Looking at the old box.)* Pops, what is all this stuff?

WILLIAM. Oh, I found it upstairs. I was just going through it trying to organize things around here. *(Ennis starts looking at the things.)*

ENNIS. Pops, you found the freaky ornaments Mama put on the tree.

MALCOLM. I like those ornaments.

ENNIS. You like black people hanging from your Christmas tree?

MALCOLM. I didn't look at it like that. I liked them because Mama liked them. *(Ennis picks up the piece of paper William had taken out of the box.)*

ENNIS. Hey, look at this!

WILLIAM. What's that?

ENNIS. You don't remember this? I drew this in fourth grade, I think.

MALCOLM. Yeah, that's the picture of a cockroach.

ENNIS. It's a dinosaur. A triceratops to be exact.

MALCOLM. It looks like a cockroach to me. It has antennae and everything. Dinosaurs don't have antennae.

WILLIAM. Antennae?

ENNIS. Tell me you just didn't say antennae.

MALCOLM. Yes, I did, because that's the proper pronunciation.

ENNIS. Doesn't matter how you say it because those are horns, man. You can tell because … you know what. I'm not talking to you right now. *(William tries to turn on the stove but is having problems seeing the settings on the dial.)* You sure you don't want someone to help you with that, Pops?

WILLIAM. I'm just being extra careful. If you want to help me, keep looking through that box, Ennis. I was going to give you those shirts your mama made. I figured you and your new family could use them.

MALCOLM. That's nice, Pops. *(Ennis looks at the shirts. His cell phone rings, he silences it again, and then checks it.)*

WILLIAM. The baby's shirt is six months, so you might have to wait a while.

MALCOLM. Maybe not too long. Little Brendon is already getting big.

WILLIAM. How is my grandbaby doing? *(Ennis, preoccupied with his cell phone, doesn't answer.)* Son!

ENNIS. Huh?

WILLIAM. My grandbaby, how's he doing?

ENNIS. He's fine, Pops. Eats half of the day. Sleeps the other half. Pisses and poops through thirty dollars of diapers every week.

WILLIAM. But other than that, it's great. Being a dad, right. *(Ennis is still looking at his cell phone.)*

ENNIS. It's unbelievable.

MALCOLM. You know if you just pick up the phone, then she'll probably stop calling.

ENNIS. I don't want to start talking to her, until you and me finish our conversation.

WILLIAM. What conversation? *(William isn't looking and the stove has caught the bottom of his shirt on fire.)*

ENNIS. Pops, your shirt!

WILLIAM. What?

MALCOLM. Shit.

WILLIAM. Whoa! *(Malcolm and Ennis rush over to William.)* Help!

MALCOLM. Move to the sink, Pops. Move! *(They all move to the sink and douse William's shirt with water.)*

38

ENNIS. I think we got it.

MALCOLM. Are you alright?

WILLIAM. I'm fine. I might have burned my hand a little, but nothing bad.

MALCOLM. Let me take a look at you.

WILLIAM. It's just my hand.

MALCOLM. Yeah, but we should make sure you didn't burn …

WILLIAM. Malcolm, I've lost my sense of sight, not touch. *(William sits. He rubs his hand.)*

ENNIS. I know you want to, Pops, but you can't do things like you use to.

WILLIAM. I was doing okay until then. I just got distracted. *(William is now rubbing his shoulder and neck, too.)*

MALCOLM. Look, if you want, we can make your meals in the morning. We'll put them in the fridge and they'll be ready when you want.

WILLIAM. Now I have to eat cold lunches.

ENNIS. You could microwave them, Pops.

WILLIAM. Cold or microwaved, huh? That's what I get.

MALCOLM. We're just trying to come up with ways to make this easier on you.

WILLIAM. Thank you, but I know all the ways to make it easier on me. Yes, you could cook for me. You could clean for me. You can give me my shots. In a few years when my balance starts to go, you can help me walk across the room. After my muscles get too weak, you can give me a bath and help me use the restroom. I've talked to the doctors and I know what's happening to me. I know all the ways to make it easier on me, but I don't want easy. You know what I want?

MALCOLM. What?

WILLIAM. I want things back to the way they were. I want to care for myself. I want to work. I'd put in sixty hours a week. I'd do my normal forty at Randy's and then I worked around the neighborhood at night and on the weekends. It wasn't too many brothers in heating and cooling so I was always busy. If somebody's furnace was screwed up, they'd call me. If somebody needed an air conditioner put in, I was on it. I wouldn't charge anybody more than they could pay, because that ain't right. Hell, one time Ms. Moore didn't have any money, but her heat wouldn't come on. I get over there, fix the problem, and this woman hands me a smoked opossum. I was kind of leery at first, but that thing wasn't bad. Hell, you and Ennis damn near ate half of it.

MALCOLM. You told us it was turkey.

WILLIAM. You wouldn't have touched it if I had told the truth. Look, the point is that I worked hard. I woke up every morning before God Himself. Didn't matter if I was sick, if it was snowing outside, I was out doing what I had to do. I couldn't wait for the day that I could sit back, relax, do nothing all day, take it easy. Well easy ain't what I thought it was gonna be. *(William rubs his hand.)*

MALCOLM. Some burn cream might help your hand.

ENNIS. I doubt we have any.

MALCOLM. We might. Check the other bathroom.

ENNIS. Why can't you?

WILLIAM. Don't worry about it. The pain in my neck distracts me from the pain in my hand.

MALCOLM. What's the matter with your neck?

WILLIAM. I've been sore all day. I might have to double up on those pain shots.

MALCOLM. I already gave you one this morning, so you can't take another until tonight. You're not on the same meds as before.

WILLIAM. And as bad as my memory is, I can't remember all of them.

MALCOLM. You have to. Look, you take three types of MS pills. And some painkillers. Strong painkillers. You can't take too much.

ENNIS. You want me to finish making you lunch?

WILLIAM. No, I'll just go lay down. It's probably safer that way.

ENNIS. You've been stuck here for days. How about I take you out? Maybe go see the baby.

WILLIAM. You don't have to work?

ENNIS. I took off today. We can even grab something to eat at Sharon's. *(William gets up and slowly walks towards the stairs.)*

WILLIAM. I get to see my grandbaby and eat at Sharon's. I can't turn that down.

ENNIS. Just change that shirt.

WILLIAM. I'll be right down. *(William slowly exits upstairs.)*

MALCOLM. He's getting worse.

ENNIS. When did you come to that conclusion? Before he tried to fricassee himself on the stove or after he was two-stepping with a garden gnome?

MALCOLM. I could care less if he was dancing with Stubby. I actually enjoyed that. He might be dying but he's not dead yet.

ENNIS. Then why are you treating him like he is?

MALCOLM. Excuse me?

ENNIS. That place we went to today, that nursing home.

MALCOLM. It's assisted living.

ENNIS. Bullshit! More like assisted dying.

MALCOLM. I'm just making sure we look at every option.

ENNIS. It smelled, Malcolm. The whole place smelled like a bathroom. Then the nurses up front kept bragging about the great security. They lock the doors from the inside so the patients can't get out. That's their security. You have to share a bedroom that's no bigger than a closet. But I barely noticed all that because I was constantly distracted by the people screaming.

MALCOLM. Thank you, Ennis. I was there with you. I saw the same thing.

ENNIS. I don't know if you did. Did you see the food? It looks like stuff I wouldn't feed a dog I didn't like.

MALCOLM. Okay, it was the worst we've seen, but it's not the only. The place in Bonner Springs wasn't too bad.

ENNIS. But it wasn't much better. And I'd have to drive damn near an hour every time I want to see him.

MALCOLM. We haven't looked in Johnson County yet.

ENNIS. That's because we know we can't afford it.

MALCOLM. Well, what else are we supposed to do, Ennis?

ENNIS. I've been telling you for months what we should do.

MALCOLM. No, you've been telling me for months what I should do. *(Ennis' phone rings again.)* Your phone is ringing.

ENNIS. No, it's not. *(Ennis silences the phone.)*

MALCOLM. You need to answer that phone, Ennis.

ENNIS. Don't worry about my phone.

MALCOLM. I'm not. I'm worried about Tammy and the baby because nobody else seems to be.

ENNIS. I thought we were discussing our father.

MALCOLM. I told you that you didn't have to come with me this morning. I could have determined the condition of that place by myself. We've been done for over an hour and you're still hanging around here.

ENNIS. You just heard me tell Pops we're getting ready to go see the baby.

MALCOLM. I can take him. Just like the last few times you've picked up Pops to see the baby. You're just making excuses for not wanting to be at home. And your phone keeps ringing, but you just ignore her.

ENNIS. Because I already know what she's going to say. I don't feel like being bitched at over the phone and at home. I'll just take it all in one lump sum when I see her. What's the big deal anyway?

MALCOLM. Tammy called here last night.

ENNIS. Oh yeah.

MALCOLM. She said you told her you were going to be here.

ENNIS. I changed my mind.

MALCOLM. Then where were you?

ENNIS. You ain't the FBI. I ain't got to answer you.

MALCOLM. Were you cheating?

ENNIS. Are you serious?

MALCOLM. Tammy thinks you are.

ENNIS. Okay. I was out with the boys.

MALCOLM. I don't believe you.

ENNIS. I don't give a shit.

MALCOLM. Tell me where you were, then.

ENNIS. I'm not telling you a thing.

MALCOLM. Tell me something.

ENNIS. What? That I don't want to be at home with my baby and Tammy? I don't. And you know what, that doesn't make me a bad person. If I didn't take care of them, that would make me a bad person. If I beat them, that would make me a bad person. Or maybe if I didn't love them. But I love them. I do. It's just between them and Pops and you and work and everything else I … it's too much. Sometimes I got to do whatever I need to do for me. You can't get mad at me for that.

MALCOLM. Why? You've been mad at me for wanting to do the same thing.

ENNIS. If you're talking about what I think you're talking about. No, it's not the same.

MALCOLM. You have to do whatever you need to do, no matter what. That's what you said. That's what you were doing last night.

ENNIS. One night every once in a while is different than five or six years. *(William begins coming down the stairs, unseen by his sons.)* You doing what you want to do involves you living some dream while our father rots in a nursing home. *(Ennis and Malcolm see their father.)*

WILLIAM. Don't worry. I really wasn't listening. I guess my hearing is going too.

ENNIS. No, you need to hear this, Pops. Listen to Malcolm's big plans for you. He calls it assisted living. I call it a shithole.

MALCOLM. You know damn well those aren't my plans.

ENNIS. What are your plans then, Malcolm? I think we've waited long enough.

MALCOLM. Pops, don't forget those shirts for Ennis and Tammy. Give Brendon a hug for me.

ENNIS. We're not going yet. We're waiting to hear your decision.

WILLIAM. Maybe we should go now. I want to see as much of my grandson as I can.

ENNIS. This won't take long, Pops. All Malcolm has to do is say, "I'm staying" or "I'm going."

MALCOLM. I can't do this now, Ennis.

ENNIS. I don't understand what the big decision is. I never have. I know you care about this family. I know you see how sick Pops is. I know you see how selfish it would be to go. I think you see all this and for some reason we're still waiting. I don't understand.

MALCOLM. Let me explain it to you. I'm stuck. I bet you understand that. I'm stuck. Just like Pops got stuck with this illness. Just like you're stuck in a life you hate. Just like everybody in the neighborhood. I'm stuck. And I knew it. I told myself not to come back. I knew the minute I walked in this house it was going to happen. And now I'm stuck with having to make this decision.

ENNIS. You don't have to. Just stay.

MALCOLM. No, stay or go, it doesn't matter. Either way, someone gets hurt. So I'm sorry all this has taken me longer than you would like.

ENNIS. Well, tonight I think we should help speed up the process.

MALCOLM. I don't know what you have in mind, but no thank you.

ENNIS. It'll be easy. We've been waiting all summer to finish that domino game, right. Tonight we do it. I win, you stay. You win, you go. That easy.

WILLIAM. Wait a minute. I want you two to listen to me. No one is betting on the future of this family.

ENNIS. Don't look at it as a bet. It's more like flipping a coin.

WILLIAM. Now, don't be foolish.

ENNIS. I can't wait any longer. So make up your mind tonight or we play for it.

MALCOLM. Ennis, I don't …

ENNIS. Pops, I'm going to grab the shirts and let's go.

WILLIAM. Let's all calm down for a minute.

ENNIS. Are you coming or not? As you can see, I'm not in the mood to wait.

WILLIAM. We're family. This isn't how we deal with problems.

ENNIS. Fuck it then. I'm out.

MALCOLM. Where are you going?

ENNIS. I'm going to do what I have to do. See you tonight. *(Ennis exits. Lights down. Lights up. It is later on that night. The sound of the ocean can be heard. Other than Stubby, who still stands near the couch, William is the only one there. William is sleeping on the couch. Now faint cries for help can be heard. It is a woman's voice and barely audible. William stirs a bit. The cries slowly fade and the sound of the ocean comes to a sudden stop as William awakes.)*

WILLIAM. Sonia? *(William looks around but sees no one. He rubs his shoulder and neck. William takes a look at his watch. He can't see the numbers. He pulls a magnifying glass out of his pocket and looks at his watch again.)* Well, Chauncey. Looks like it's just us again. *(William slowly stands and walks over to the kitchen. He opens the refrigerator and uses the magnifying glass as he peers in. He pulls out the container of chocolate milk.)* I think this stuff is going bad. *(William looks at the date with the magnifying glass.)* Not yet. You want a glass? *(Stubby doesn't answer.)* I'll pour you one anyway. *(William pours two glasses of chocolate milk.)* I'm the only one in the house that drinks this stuff. If Sonia was here we'd be going through a carton every other day. A lot of things would be different if she was around. *(William walks over to the couch, puts the two glasses down on the coffee table, and begins to roll up his sleeve.)* This house would be a little more picked up, that's for sure. The kitchen counter with the stains on it would have driven you up a wall. I mean driven her up a wall. "If I'm going to be stuck in the house, then I'm going to be stuck in a clean house." That's what she'd say. *(William takes out his medicine and gets his needle ready with help of the magnifying glass.)* There'd be more music playing. Sonia couldn't stand the silence so she'd always blast the radio, and sing and dance around the house. She loved sweets, too. Couldn't tell by looking at her, but she did. The house always smelled like whatever she was cooking. It was great to come home to. Even after you got sick, you didn't get all depressed like me. No, you kept making sweets and singing and dancing. Up until the end. You're so strong. Hell, my eye gets crossed and I cover it up. When you lost your hair, you went out for

44

Halloween dressed like a Milk Dud. I'm stuck in this house and I feel like I'm going nuts. I have two sons I want to take care of but instead they're taking care of me. You wouldn't have let that happen. You're stronger than me. I mean, she was stronger than me. *(The needle is ready. William gives himself a shot.)* I'm sorry. I know you didn't come over here to listen to me whine. I'm sure you have your own drama. *(William puts away the needle and medicine.)* Right, Chauncey. A handsome gnome like you probably has his fair share of the ladies. And that means you've had your fair share of drama. So let's forget about our problems tonight and let's just lose ourselves in a game of dominoes. How about we play a hand? *(William goes over to the table and sits. Stubby doesn't move.)* What's wrong? You know how to play, don't you? *(Stubby doesn't answer.)* You can't be any worse than Ennis and Malcolm when they first started playing. Let me give you a few pointers. We always play seven or nines. That means each player starts with … *(Malcolm enters from outside.)* You're back.

MALCOLM. Yeah, I had to take a drive.

WILLIAM. Are you okay?

MALCOLM. I'm fine. Ennis hasn't called, has he?

WILLIAM. No.

MALCOLM. He was pretty pissed this afternoon. I hope he wasn't serious about the domino game.

WILLIAM. We'll see about that.

MALCOLM. And what he said about me wanting to throw you away. You know I'd never do that, right?

WILLIAM. I could never ask you to stay here and take care of me either. I didn't raise you to be my nurse.

MALCOLM. I still don't know what to do. I thought about leaving and finding a way to come home every week.

WILLIAM. Every week? That's going to get expensive.

MALCOLM. I know. I've even been thinking about bringing you with me.

WILLIAM. To Connecticut?

MALCOLM. I don't want to stay here, but I don't want to leave you like this. Maybe I could get a two-bedroom. I think you'd like the East Coast.

WILLIAM. Yeah?

MALCOLM. Yeah. You'd like the beach.

WILLIAM. I've never been to the beach.

MALCOLM. I'd be willing to do this.

WILLIAM. But I'm not. I can't, Malcolm. I'd miss this house. Your life may be somewhere else, but my life is here.

MALCOLM. I can understand that.

WILLIAM. Look, we've made a lot of tough decisions in this family. When you were only four or five years old, I was laid off. There was another company that offered me the same job but for less money. I decided to wait it out until something opened up with Randy. Money was going to be tight and I didn't know how your mama was going to handle it. But she had my back. She became a light Nazi. If you weren't in the room, the lights had to be off. When we did go somewhere, we took the bus and we ate as cheap as we could. I'm talking hamburger hash, homemade rolls, peanut butter spoons for dessert.

MALCOLM. I remember peanut butter spoons. You dip a spoon in peanut butter and you lick it.

WILLIAM. That's right.

MALCOLM. I loved those things. I didn't know we ate them because we were broke.

WILLIAM. That's because me and your mama wouldn't let you think of our family as poor. We weren't ashamed. We didn't want you thinking you were beneath anybody. We — *(Ennis enters. He is wearing his work uniform, which is simply a pair of jeans and a T-shirt that says "Lord of the Wings." All three men are silent for a moment.)*

ENNIS. Don't stop talking because of me. Unless you two were sitting around here in awkward silence before I came in.

MALCOLM. You're wearing your work T-shirt.

ENNIS. Unfortunately.

MALCOLM. I thought you were off today.

ENNIS. So did I. But I guess I was wrong.

WILLIAM. What happened?

ENNIS. Well, Pops. I got fucked. And not in the good way. I got fucked because I'm a nice person and a hard worker. I went to the restaurant to talk to someone. That's it. I was picking up some batteries at Target, and you know Lord of the Wings is right next door. I knew my boy Leon was working today, and our punk-ass manger didn't give him the days off that he wanted, so I told him I'd switch a few shifts with him. I go in to talk to Leon. I thought that I'd be in and out, but oh no.

MALCOLM. Your manager made you work.

ENNIS. I wasn't in the building for longer than a minute before he came down my neck, talking about two of his line cooks quit so he needed me to work tonight.

WILLIAM. Why didn't you say no?

ENNIS. I did, Pops. But this mothafucka is ruthless. He said since I was a trainer I had different responsibilities than everybody else. Told me if I couldn't handle those responsibilities then he would find somebody who could.

MALCOLM. That's not fair.

ENNIS. I know.

MALCOLM. You should have told him to kiss your ass.

ENNIS. Oh, I did better than that. I walked up to him very calmly. Threw a dirty dishrag in his face. I told him he could take my job and shove it up his fat, racist ass. Then I ran out into the restaurant and bitch-slapped all the customers. I told them to eat at home or our food would give them massive heart attacks. Then I went back into the kitchen, opened up the smoker, and pissed on every rack of ribs in there. As I walked out the back door, I high-fived all my ex-coworkers. Then I snapped back into reality, and I was still standing there in front of my manager, and he was handing me a work T-shirt and an apron. And I didn't say a word.

MALCOLM. Why?

ENNIS. Because I need that job. I need money. My broke-ology degree isn't bringing in the big bucks like I thought it would. I'd love to quit. I daydream about it. But as we've discussed, I'm stuck. *(Pause.)* Well, enough small talk. I believe we have a game to finish.

MALCOLM. It doesn't look like we have to.

ENNIS. So you know what you're doing.

MALCOLM. Yeah.

ENNIS. And when did you figure this out?

MALCOLM. Just now.

ENNIS. Well, don't disappoint me. *(Pause.)*

MALCOLM. I'm not staying. I'm going back. *(Pause.)*

ENNIS. And you honestly believe that's the right thing?

MALCOLM. I have no idea. But that's what I'm going to do. You wanted me to make a decision and now I have.

WILLIAM. Good, let's play bones.

ENNIS. Well, I must admit. I'm a little bit surprised. You come back here and see every reason in the world to stay, but you still leave.

MALCOLM. I don't expect you to understand.

ENNIS. Well, help me to. Explain it.

WILLIAM. No, Malcolm is leaving. He shouldn't have to explain a thing.

ENNIS. So you're okay with this?

WILLIAM. Yes, I am. I was hoping that's what he would say.

ENNIS. You were hoping he would say that he was leaving us. That he was putting himself over the family. You were hoping he would say, "So long, Pops. Have fun rotting away in the nursing home."

WILLIAM. If that's what it came down to, then yes. I would do that for him because he's my son. I'm not standing in his way and I'll be damned if you do either.

ENNIS. So that's it.

MALCOLM. That's it.

ENNIS. Then why am I still here? *(Ennis turns to leave.)*

WILLIAM. Because we have a domino game to play.

ENNIS. Malcolm just made his decision. No need to play anymore.

WILLIAM. I'm not talking about that. Do you think I was going to let you two decide our future with dominoes? I just want to play a game.

ENNIS. I'm not in the mood.

WILLIAM. Get over it. We're going to finish this game.

ENNIS. I'm not playing dominoes tonight.

WILLIAM. Yes, you are! Yes, you are, Ennis. That's all I'm asking for, and I think I've earned it. We're all sitting down tonight together as a family, and we are finishing this game! *(William drops to his chair and grabs his arm. He is in pain.)*

MALCOLM. Pops, what's wrong? *(Malcolm rushes over to William.)* Pops.

WILLIAM. I'm fine.

MALCOLM. Then what in the hell was that?

WILLIAM. Just a little pain.

MALCOLM. That didn't look like a little.

ENNIS. Have you taken your shot tonight? *(Pause.)*

WILLIAM. I don't think so.

MALCOLM. You don't think so? I know your memory is not always the best, but you have to be sure on this.

WILLIAM. I'm sure. I haven't taken any shots tonight. Just the one this morning.

ENNIS. I'll get it ready for you.

WILLIAM. Actually, let me do that.

48

MALCOLM. Just let Ennis set it up.

WILLIAM. No. You're leaving and Ennis has the baby. I've got to be able to do this by myself. So just hand me the medicine. *(Ennis does as his father says. William gets the needle ready.)* Thank you. Now, both of you sit. *(Malcolm and Ennis don't move.)* Come on, sit. I'll do this, we'll play one quick hand, and you can go on about your business. *(Malcolm and Ennis reluctantly sit. The three men are silent for a moment.)* I had a dream a little while ago. I was napping before you two got here. We were in a boat out on the ocean.

ENNIS. You told us this before.

WILLIAM. Did I?

MALCOLM. Yeah, he's right.

ENNIS. Me, you and Mama in that boat. The boat starts to sink and we can't swim, but you can only save one person.

WILLIAM. Did I tell you what your mama was wearing?

MALCOLM. That green dress.

WILLIAM. I guess I did tell you that. I shouldn't be surprised. I've had the dream damn near every night this summer, so it's been on my mind a lot. I don't know what it means. But today it was different. It was the same up until the end. Normally I wake up before I have to choose who to save. But today I made a choice.

ENNIS. Who'd you save?

WILLIAM. I saved you. Then I swam back out and drowned with my wife. *(The needle is ready. William gives himself a shot.)* Maybe I've gone crazy. Or maybe I just miss your mama.

MALCOLM. I know what you mean.

ENNIS. We all do.

WILLIAM. That's good to hear. Let's play. *(William puts away the needle as Malcolm stirs the dominoes. All three men pull nine dominoes.)* Who's got the big six?

ENNIS. Wait a minute. Pops, I know you really want to finish the game. And I would sit here and do that, despite the fact that I'm still a little pissed off. But Tammy's been at home with the baby all day, because I was at work.

WILLIAM. Oh, yeah.

ENNIS. I really do want to play, but …

WILLIAM. No, you're right. You should go.

MALCOLM. How about this? Everybody turn over one domino. The biggest bone wins.

ENNIS. That ain't dominoes.

MALCOLM. I know, but it's something.

WILLIAM. Yeah, that'll work.

ENNIS. Okay, what you boys got? *(Ennis turns over a bone.)* Oh, the five-three. Not bad. *(Malcolm turns over a bone.)* Deuce-one. Bad. *(William turns over a bone.)*

WILLIAM. What do I have?

ENNIS. You got the double three.

MALCOLM. Ennis.

ENNIS. Just playing. It's the double five. You win.

MALCOLM. Good game, Pops.

ENNIS. I'm out.

WILLIAM. Oh, one last thing before you go.

ENNIS. Pops, I have to get home.

WILLIAM. I know. It'll only be a few minutes.

ENNIS. What? *(William points to Stubby.)*

WILLIAM. Take him back.

ENNIS. Tonight?

WILLIAM. Ms. Moore will be asleep. She'll never know you were the ones who stole Chauncey in the first place.

MALCOLM. His name is Stubby.

WILLIAM. Whatever his name is, you put him back. Together. *(Malcolm and Ennis look at Stubby.)* The longer you wait, the longer it takes. *(Malcolm and Ennis walk over to Stubby. They kneel down and grab him.)*

MALCOLM. On three. One. Two. Three. *(They lift Stubby and head towards the door.)*

WILLIAM. Be safe out there.

ENNIS. You gonna make me carry this thing backwards all the way there?

MALCOLM. We can switch off halfway.

ENNIS. And damn. Why you holding him so high? You making us work harder.

MALCOLM. It ain't that bad. You're just bitching because you're mad.

ENNIS. Hell, yeah I am, but I guess there ain't shit we can do about it.

MALCOLM. No. We just gotta find a way to make it work. *(Ennis and Malcolm leave with Stubby. William watches them through the window. He then goes over to the stereo and rewinds his tape. He presses play. The Temptations-like song from earlier starts to* *play.* * *He sings along. William walks over to the table. He gets the medicine case and his magnifying glass. William sits on the couch. He gets the needle ready for another shot. William gives himself a shot. He puts away the medicine and then lies down on the couch. After a few minutes he closes his eyes and drifts away. Sonia enters from upstairs. She gently wakes him, grabs his hand and they walk upstairs together. Blackout.)*

End of Play

---

* See Special Note on Songs and Recordings on copyright page.

PROPERTY LIST

T-shirts
Paint, paintbrush
Cup of coffee
Container of chocolate milk, glasses
Dominoes
Medicine, syringe
Container of orange juice
Large garden gnome
Notebook, pen
Straight razor
Towel
Keys
Box of random items, including ornaments, papers, T-shirts,
    cassette tape
Magnifying glass
Radio

SOUND EFFECTS

Cell phone rings
Motown-like music
Sound of the ocean, faint cries for help

NEW PLAYS

★ **A CIVIL WAR CHRISTMAS: AN AMERICAN MUSICAL CELEBRA-TION by Paula Vogel, music by Daryl Waters.** It's 1864, and Washington, D.C. is settling down to the coldest Christmas Eve in years. Intertwining many lives, this musical shows us that the gladness of one's heart is the best gift of all. "Boldly inventive theater, warm and affecting." *–Talkin' Broadway.* "Crisp strokes of dialogue." *–NY Times.* [12M, 5W] ISBN: 978-0-8222-2361-0

★ **SPEECH & DEBATE by Stephen Karam.** Three teenage misfits in Salem, Oregon discover they are linked by a sex scandal that's rocked their town. "Savvy comedy." *–Variety.* "Hilarious, cliché-free, and immensely entertaining." *–NY Times.* "A strong, rangy play." *–NY Newsday.* [2M, 2W] ISBN: 978-0-8222-2286-6

★ **DIVIDING THE ESTATE by Horton Foote.** Matriarch Stella Gordon is determined not to divide her 100-year-old Texas estate, despite her family's declining wealth and the looming financial crisis. But her three children have another plan. "Goes for laughs and succeeds." *–NY Daily News.* "The theatrical equivalent of a page-turner." *–Bloomberg.com.* [4M, 9W] ISBN: 978-0-8222-2398-6

★ **WHY TORTURE IS WRONG, AND THE PEOPLE WHO LOVE THEM by Christopher Durang.** Christopher Durang turns political humor upside down with this raucous and provocative satire about America's growing homeland "insecurity." "A smashing new play." *–NY Observer.* "You may laugh yourself silly." *–Bloomberg News.* [4M, 3W] ISBN: 978-0-8222-2401-3

★ **FIFTY WORDS by Michael Weller.** While their nine-year-old son is away for the night on his first sleepover, Adam and Jan have an evening alone together, beginning a suspenseful nightlong roller-coaster ride of revelation, rancor, passion and humor. "Mr. Weller is a bold and productive dramatist." *–NY Times.* [1M, 1W] ISBN: 978-0-8222-2348-1

★ **BECKY'S NEW CAR by Steven Dietz.** Becky Foster is caught in middle age, middle management and in a middling marriage—with no prospects for change on the horizon. Then one night a socially inept and grief-struck millionaire stumbles into the car dealership where Becky works. "Gently and consistently funny." *–Variety.* "Perfect blend of hilarious comedy and substantial weight." *–Broadway Hour.* [4M, 3W] ISBN: 978-0-8222-2393-1

DRAMATISTS PLAY SERVICE, INC.
440 Park Avenue South, New York, NY 10016 212-683-8960 Fax 212-213-1539
postmaster@dramatists.com www.dramatists.com

NEW PLAYS

★ **AT HOME AT THE ZOO by Edward Albee.** Edward Albee delves deeper into his play THE ZOO STORY by adding a first act, HOMELIFE, which precedes Peter's fateful meeting with Jerry on a park bench in Central Park. "An essential and heartening experience." –*NY Times.* "Darkly comic and thrilling." –*Time Out.* "Genuinely fascinating." –*Journal News.* [2M, 1W] ISBN: 978-0-8222-2317-7

★ **PASSING STRANGE book and lyrics by Stew, music by Stew and Heidi Rodewald, created in collaboration with Annie Dorsen.** A daring musical about a young bohemian that takes you from black middle-class America to Amsterdam, Berlin and beyond on a journey towards personal and artistic authenticity. "Fresh, exuberant, bracingly inventive, bitingly funny, and full of heart." –*NY Times.* "The freshest musical in town!" –*Wall Street Journal.* "Excellent songs and a vulnerable heart." –*Variety.* [4M, 3W] ISBN: 978-0-8222-2400-6

★ **REASONS TO BE PRETTY by Neil LaBute.** Greg really, truly adores his girlfriend, Steph. Unfortunately, he also thinks she has a few physical imperfections, and when he mentions them, all hell breaks loose. "Tight, tense and emotionally true." –*Time Magazine.* "Lively and compulsively watchable." –*The Record.* [2M, 2W] ISBN: 978-0-8222-2394-8

★ **OPUS by Michael Hollinger.** With only a few days to rehearse a grueling Beethoven masterpiece, a world-class string quartet struggles to prepare their highest-profile performance ever—a televised ceremony at the White House. "Intimate, intense and profoundly moving." –*Time Out.* "Worthy of scores of bravissimos." –*BroadwayWorld.com.* [4M, 1W] ISBN: 978-0-8222-2363-4

★ **BECKY SHAW by Gina Gionfriddo.** When an evening calculated to bring happiness takes a dark turn, crisis and comedy ensue in this wickedly funny play that asks what we owe the people we love and the strangers who land on our doorstep. "As engrossing as it is ferociously funny." –*NY Times.* "Gionfriddo is some kind of genius." –*Variety.* [2M, 3W] ISBN: 978-0-8222-2402-0

★ **KICKING A DEAD HORSE by Sam Shepard.** Hobart Struther's horse has just dropped dead. In an eighty-minute monologue, he discusses what path brought him here in the first place, the fate of his marriage, his career, politics and eventually the nature of the universe. "Deeply instinctual and intuitive." –*NY Times.* "The brilliance is in the infinite reverberations Shepard extracts from his simple metaphor." –*TheaterMania.* [1M, 1W] ISBN: 978-0-8222-2336-8

DRAMATISTS PLAY SERVICE, INC.
440 Park Avenue South, New York, NY 10016 212-683-8960 Fax 212-213-1539
postmaster@dramatists.com www.dramatists.com

NEW PLAYS

★ **AUGUST: OSAGE COUNTY by Tracy Letts.** WINNER OF THE 2008 PULITZER PRIZE AND TONY AWARD. When the large Weston family reunites after Dad disappears, their Oklahoma homestead explodes in a maelstrom of repressed truths and unsettling secrets. "Fiercely funny and bitingly sad." –*NY Times.* "Ferociously entertaining." –*Variety.* "A hugely ambitious, highly combustible saga." –*NY Daily News.* [6M, 7W] ISBN: 978-0-8222-2300-9

★ **RUINED by Lynn Nottage.** WINNER OF THE 2009 PULITZER PRIZE. Set in a small mining town in Democratic Republic of Congo, RUINED is a haunting, probing work about the resilience of the human spirit during times of war. "A full-immersion drama of shocking complexity and moral ambiguity." –*Variety.* "Sincere, passionate, courageous." –*Chicago Tribune.* [8M, 4W] ISBN: 978-0-8222-2390-0

★ **GOD OF CARNAGE by Yasmina Reza, translated by Christopher Hampton.** WINNER OF THE 2009 TONY AWARD. A playground altercation between boys brings together their Brooklyn parents, leaving the couples in tatters as the rum flows and tensions explode. "Satisfyingly primitive entertainment." –*NY Times.* "Elegant, acerbic, entertainingly fueled on pure bile." –*Variety.* [2M, 2W] ISBN: 978-0-8222-2399-3

★ **THE SEAFARER by Conor McPherson.** Sharky has returned to Dublin to look after his irascible, aging brother. Old drinking buddies Ivan and Nicky are holed up at the house too, hoping to play some cards. But with the arrival of a stranger from the distant past, the stakes are raised ever higher. "Dark and enthralling Christmas fable." –*NY Times.* "A timeless classic." –*Hollywood Reporter.* [5M] ISBN: 978-0-8222-2284-2

★ **THE NEW CENTURY by Paul Rudnick.** When the playwright is Paul Rudnick, expectations are geared for a play both hilarious and smart, and this provocative and outrageous comedy is no exception. "The one-liners fly like rockets." –*NY Times.* "The funniest playwright around." –*Journal News.* [2M, 3W] ISBN: 978-0-8222-2315-3

★ **SHIPWRECKED! AN ENTERTAINMENT—THE AMAZING ADVENTURES OF LOUIS DE ROUGEMONT (AS TOLD BY HIMSELF) by Donald Margulies.** The amazing story of bravery, survival and celebrity that left nineteenth-century England spellbound. Dare to be whisked away. "A deft, literate narrative." –*LA Times.* "Springs to life like a theatrical pop-up book." –*NY Times.* [2M, 1W] ISBN: 978-0-8222-2341-2

DRAMATISTS PLAY SERVICE, INC.
440 Park Avenue South, New York, NY 10016 212-683-8960 Fax 212-213-1539
postmaster@dramatists.com www.dramatists.com